Original title:
A Stronger Heart

Copyright © 2024 Swan Charm
All rights reserved.

Author: Sara Säde
ISBN HARDBACK: 978-9916-79-000-7
ISBN PAPERBACK: 978-9916-79-001-4
ISBN EBOOK: 978-9916-79-002-1

Harmony in Healing

In quiet breaths, the heart unveils,
Soft whispers calm, where silence prevails.
Nature sings with vibrant hue,
In every tear, a strength anew.

Gentle hands mend what is torn,
Through darkest nights, new hopes are born.
With each step, the soul takes flight,
In harmony, we find the light.

The Symphony of Survival

Life's orchestration, a grand design,
Each note a story, intertwined.
Through trials faced, the courage swells,
In echoes of strength, the spirit dwells.

With each crescendo, we rise and fall,
Resilient hearts, we hear the call.
Bound by struggles, yet we stand,
Together, united, hand in hand.

Embers of Resilience

In ashes cold, a spark ignites,
From shattered dreams, the flame invites.
Through storms we weather, fierce and bold,
Each ember whispers stories told.

Hope rekindles with every breath,
From shadows deep, we conquer death.
In the fire's glow, we find our way,
And rise anew, with each new day.

Unbreakable Spirit

Silent battles fought within,
From doubts and fears, we learn to win.
A heart that beats, though bruised and worn,
In every challenge, a strength reborn.

We carry scars like badges worn,
In every tear, new hope is sworn.
For every fall, we rise again,
An unbreakable spirit, free from pain.

Rebirth in Stillness

In quiet hours, the heart resets,
Whispers of change in gentle breaths.
The world slows down, the mind finds peace,
A garden blooms where doubts release.

Soft petals unfurl in the dawn's embrace,
Color weaves softly through time and space.
A soul emerges, cast away the gloom,
With every heartbeat, new life will bloom.

In stillness, shadows begin to fade,
Parting the clouds, a promise is made.
Roots deepen firmly within the earth,
In silence, we find our true rebirth.

Fortifying the Soul

Brick by brick, we build our walls,
Strong foundations through life's vast calls.
Every challenge shapes our core,
In trials, we find strength and more.

Resilience flows like a river wide,
In the depths, our courage will abide.
We rise from ashes, fierce and bold,
In unity, our spirits consoled.

With every scar, a story we weave,
In the fabric of life, we learn to believe.
Fortified hearts can weather the storm,
Together we rise, united and warm.

The Beat of Strength

Hear the pulse of the earth below,
In its rhythm, let your spirit grow.
Each heartbeat echoes tales untold,
In this dance of life, be brave and bold.

Strength lies not just in the might,
But in the heart that fights for the light.
With every struggle, we learn to stand,
Side by side, we'll face what's planned.

Let the beat guide your steady feet,
In the journey's march, find your heartbeat.
Together we rise, our voices blend,
In the flow of strength, we find no end.

Songs of Survival

In the shadows, where hope feels lost,
A tune emerges, no matter the cost.
Whispers of courage pierce the night,
In shared songs of survival, we find our light.

The melody soars through thick and thin,
Binding our wounds and healing within.
With every chorus, we learn to fight,
In harmony, we reclaim our right.

Each note a reminder of battles fought,
In the symphony of life, lessons taught.
Together we rise, through sorrow and glee,
In the songs of survival, we are free.

Boundless Beats

In the rhythm of the heart,
Every beat a brand new start.
Dancing through the night sky,
Melodies that never die.

Harmony in vibrant hues,
Life's song plays with gentle cues.
Whispers of the endless flow,
Echoes of the dreams we sow.

Breathless in the magic's sway,
Lost in sound, we find our way.
Each note a spark of the divine,
Together we forever shine.

With every sound, the world awakes,
In the music, love forsakes.
Flowing rivers, wild and free,
Boundless beats, just you and me.

Reflections in the Strength

In the mirror of the soul,
Confidence is our true goal.
Strength resides within our core,
Unlocking dreams, we rise and soar.

Challenges we face each day,
In reflections, we find our way.
With courage to ignite the fire,
We reach for hope, our hearts aspire.

Moments frail, yet spirits strong,
Together we will march along.
Building bridges forged in light,
Guided by our endless fight.

What we see is what we are,
Each battle carries us far.
With wisdom in our stride, we grow,
Reflections of the strength we know.

Wings of Hope

Lifted high on wings of grace,
Hope resides in every space.
Through the storms, we learn to fly,
Painting dreams across the sky.

Each feather tells a tale of light,
Guiding hearts through darkest night.
With every challenge that we face,
Resilience finds its rightful place.

Wings outstretched, we break the chains,
In the struggle, freedom reigns.
With love as strong as rising tide,
Together we shall turn the tide.

In the skies where dreams awaken,
Our spirits soar, no hearts forsaken.
Hand in hand through paths unknown,
On wings of hope, we find our home.

The Pulse of Perseverance

In the echoes of our strive,
Perseverance keeps us alive.
With every step, we claim our truth,
The journey honoring our youth.

Through the shadows, we will tread,
Fighting doubts that might be fed.
Each heartbeat fuels the drive within,
Resilience growing, we begin.

Facing storms with steady gaze,
We navigate the toughest maze.
With courage as our guiding star,
We chart the course, we rise afar.

In the rhythm of our quest,
We find purpose, we find rest.
Unyielding spirit, strong and free,
The pulse of perseverance is key.

The Heart's Forge

In the glow of embers bright,
Passion dances through the night.
Shaping dreams with every strike,
Anvil sings and hopes ignite.

Steel of spirit, forged in fire,
Crafting will through pure desire.
Hammer down, the pressure yields,
Tales of strength the heart reveals.

With each clamor, sparks will fly,
Echoes of the dreams we try.
In this forge, we fight and mold,
Stories of the brave and bold.

Beats of Courage

In shadows deep, a heartbeat thrums,
A whisper fierce, though silence hums.
Each pulse a promise, strong and clear,
Courage whispers, 'Face your fear.'

With every step upon this ground,
A symphony of strength is found.
Brave the storm, the winds will roar,
For within, the heart will soar.

Against the odds, we rise and stand,
A legacy of hope in hand.
Through trials fierce, our spirits dance,
In beats of courage, we advance.

Pulse of Perseverance

Through struggles vast, the journey winds,
With steady pulse, the spirit finds.
In moments dark, when doubts arise,
Perseverance shines, and never dies.

Each setback carved, a lesson learned,
A flicker caught, a fire burned.
With grit and grace, we push ahead,
In every step, our dreams are fed.

No storm can break the will inside,
In unity, we'll turn the tide.
For every challenge, we endure,
In the pulse of life, we are sure.

Wings of Fortitude

Lifted high on wings of grace,
Fortitude finds its rightful place.
Through trials faced and battles fought,
Strength is woven, deeply sought.

With every flight, we face the sky,
Dreams unbound, we learn to fly.
Through storms that shake the very ground,
In resilience, hope is found.

So spread your wings, embrace the day,
With every challenge, find your way.
United hearts, together soar,
For in fortitude, we're evermore.

Into the Wild Unknown

Beneath the stars, the whispers call,
Through tangled woods, I dare to fall.
To seek the face of shadows lost,
Each step I take, I count the cost.

A river sings of secrets old,
In every bend, a tale unfolds.
The rustling leaves, a voice sublime,
In wild embrace, I lose all time.

Mountains rise, fierce and grand,
I stand in awe at nature's hand.
With every breath, I feel alive,
In endless wild, my spirit thrives.

The path uncertain, but heart so bold,
Adventures call, a quest untold.
Through realm of dreams, I dare to roam,
In wild unknown, I find my home.

Sonnet of Endurance

Through storms that rage and skies of gray,
I walk the line, I choose to stay.
Each trial faced, a step I climb,
In moments dark, I find my rhyme.

For every tear that falls like rain,
A seed of hope will break the chain.
In silent battles, courage grows,
With every wound, my spirit knows.

The road is long, the night is deep,
But dreams awaken from their sleep.
With heart afire, I face the dawn,
In every heartbeat, I press on.

Through whispered doubts and hidden fears,
I gather strength from all my years.
With each new day, resolve arises,
In flames of faith, my heart surmises.

The Courage Within

When shadows creep and courage wanes,
I seek the strength amidst the pains.
Deep in my heart, a flame ignites,
A quiet roar through darkest nights.

With every fear that haunts my mind,
I search for peace, the truth to find.
In whispered doubts, my spirit cries,
To break the bonds and touch the skies.

The journey's long, but I press on,
For on the path, my fear is gone.
In every step, I learn to stand,
With courage strong, I take command.

The echoes of my past now fade,
In newfound light, my fears betrayed.
With heart of lion, firm and true,
I rise each day, to start anew.

Flames of Renewal

In ashes cold, a spark will flare,
To breathe life back, to mend the tear.
From troubles deep, a phoenix flies,
In flames of hope, the heart complies.

What once was lost, I strive to gain,
With every loss, more strength I feign.
The embers glow with stories told,
Of battles fought and spirits bold.

From darkness blooms a radiant light,
In tender hearts, we find our fight.
For every end, a chance begins,
In flames of renewal, life now spins.

With hands held high, I take my stand,
To face the world, to heal the land.
With courage forged in fire's embrace,
I rise again, and find my place.

Tides of Tenacity

In the depths of stormy seas,
Where waves of doubt crash strong,
A heart built of resolve,
Pushes forward, carries on.

With every rise and fall,
A rhythm fierce and bold,
The tides may sway and shift,
Yet steadfast dreams unfold.

In shadows where fears linger,
Hope anchors with its light,
Through every night of struggle,
Tomorrow greets the fight.

The journey's bittersweet,
But strength is forged in pain,
Each scar a testament,
To all that we maintain.

So ride the waves of courage,
Let tenacity reside,
For in the depths of tempest,
We find the will to stride.

The Armor of Love

In the quiet of the night,
When shadows softly fade,
Love wraps around the heart,
A shield that won't degrade.

Through trials and through tears,
Its strength begins to rise,
A fortress made of trust,
Reflecting endless skies.

With every whispered word,
And every shared embrace,
The armor grows more thick,
In every cherished space.

When battles rage outside,
And storms begin to roar,
Love stands firm against fears,
A guardian at the door.

So wear this armor close,
Let it your spirit lift,
For love as pure as this,
Is humanity's great gift.

Whispers of the Brave

In the shadows of the night,
Where silence seems to reign,
A voice speaks soft yet clear,
Calling forth strength from pain.

The brave may tremble deep,
Yet rise to meet the call,
With courage like a beacon,
That guides through it all.

Each heart that dares to dream,
And face the world anew,
Hears whispers in the dark,
That urge them to break through.

Standing tall and resolute,
They strive to pave the way,
For others lost in doubt,
To join in brave ballet.

So let the whispers guide,
With every step we take,
For bravery is born,
In the chances that we make.

Vibrations of Victory

In the pulse of the moment,
When triumph starts to bloom,
The air is charged with light,
Resounding in the room.

Each heartbeat tells a tale,
Of struggles faced and won,
The symphony of hope,
Plays on from dawn to sun.

Through sweat and quiet grit,
Resilience takes its stand,
In every cheering voice,
United, hand in hand.

With echoes of the past,
We rise and dare to soar,
For every trial endured,
Opens another door.

So let the world bear witness,
To this vibrant refrain,
Of victory's embrace,
And the joy that we attain.

The Weight of Strength

In the silence, shadows rise,
Carrying burdens, heavy sighs.
Yet muscle forged in tempered fire,
Awakens hope, lifts us higher.

Each trial a stone, each pain a thread,
We weave our paths with whispers said.
Together we stand, united we press,
For strength is born in the heart's caress.

With weary hands, we build our way,
Through darkest nights and longest day.
The weight we bear, a past untold,
Shapes the strength that we uphold.

In every stumble, in every fall,
Resilience sings, a rallying call.
For in the ashes, we find our might,
Turning shadows into light.

So carry the weight, let it be known,
In every heart, true strength has grown.
Together we'll rise, unbent and free,
In the weight of strength, we find unity.

The Courage to Thrive

In the depths where fears lie still,
A seed is planted with iron will.
Against the storm, we choose to fight,
The courage to thrive, a burning light.

With trembling steps, we face the dawn,
Each heartbeat sings, a promise drawn.
For living bold, we step outside,
Embracing dreams with arms spread wide.

The whispers doubt, but hope resounds,
In every struggle, victory grounds.
Through ruffles of fate, our spirits soar,
With courage, we knock on opportunity's door.

When shadows loom, let voices rise,
For in our truth, the strength defies.
In laughter, tears, we find the hive,
A collective will, the courage to thrive.

So wear your heart like battle's crest,
In vulnerability, we find our best.
For life is rich, and fear is slight,
In each of us, the courage to fight.

Echoes of the Heart

Whispers dance on gentle breeze,
Carrying tales of love with ease.
In every heartbeat, stories glide,
Echoes of the heart, forever tied.

Through laughter's joy and sorrow's sigh,
Each echo sings, we can't deny.
Together in rhythm, we find our song,
In the quiet hum, where we belong.

Moments wrapped in tender grace,
Time weaves us through this sacred space.
In every glance, connections burn,
Echoes of the heart, in waves we learn.

When silence falls and shadows creep,
The heart's echoes wake from sleep.
To find the strength in every part,
In unity, we mend the heart.

So let us cherish the sound we share,
For in the echoes, love's true dare.
Together we'll sing, never apart,
In the symphony of the heart.

The Canvas of Bravery

With colors bright, we splash the air,
On the canvas of life, we bravely dare.
Each stroke a moment, vivid and bold,
Stories of courage, etched in gold.

From shades of sorrow to joy's embrace,
We paint our journeys, no trace erased.
In every flaw, there lies a tale,
The canvas speaks where words would fail.

With brushes laden with dreams in hand,
We create a world, a vision grand.
Together we blend, our spirits rise,
In expressions of love, our courage flies.

Each layer thickens, a testament true,
To the battles fought, the triumphs too.
For bravery whispers in colors bright,
On the canvas of our shared light.

So let your heart, a palette fair,
Create a masterpiece beyond compare.
In unity, our spirits' embroidery,
Paint the bold strokes of bravery.

The Strength of Silence

In stillness lies a gentle power,
Whispers weaving through each hour.
A calm embrace, a silent plea,
Echoes of what's meant to be.

Words unspoken, secrets hold,
Stories waiting to be told.
In quietude, our hearts align,
In silence, truth begins to shine.

Beneath the noise, we find our way,
In the dark, there blooms the day.
With patience, we shall learn to hear,
The strength of silence drawing near.

So let the world around us roar,
We find our peace forevermore.
For in the hush, we learn to see,
The strength that's found in harmony.

Fables of the Fearless

Once upon a time, they dared,
With hearts ablaze, they weren't scared.
They danced with shadows, faced the night,
Their spirits soared, a fearless flight.

Each tale they spun, a spark of hope,
Through valleys deep, they learned to cope.
In every challenge, courage bloomed,
Their legacy forever loomed.

With every step, they changed the game,
Their hearts ignited, fierce with flame.
They challenged fate with every breath,
In their own way, they conquered death.

So gather round, and lend an ear,
To fables filled with joy and fear.
For in their stories, we all see,
The strength of souls that dare to be.

Weathering the Storm

Dark clouds gather, the winds will howl,
Nature's fury begins to growl.
Yet deep inside, we stand so tall,
Together we can face it all.

Raindrops pelt, the lightning strikes,
But hope ignites our inner lights.
With every crash, we're pushed and pulled,
Through trials hard, our hearts are fueled.

The tempest roars, we hold our ground,
In unity, strength can be found.
For after rain, the sun will gleam,
We'll rise again, we'll live our dream.

Hands entwined, we weather it through,
Our spirits strong, resilient too.
With whispered prayers that pierce the night,
We stand as one, prepared to fight.

Heartbeats of Freedom

In every pulse, the wild beats sound,
A call to arms, where hope is found.
With every breath, we break the chains,
In unity, our spirit reigns.

Across the fields, where dreams take flight,
With courage bold, we chase the light.
No longer bound by fears of old,
Our stories rise, our truths unfold.

In every heart, a yearning flame,
For freedom's song, we learn its name.
Together strong, we lift our voice,
In every step, we make our choice.

So let us dance beneath the sky,
With joyful hearts, we'll learn to fly.
For in our souls, the rhythm's clear,
The heartbeats of freedom, loud and near.

Heart and Heft

In the stillness, dreams take flight,
Whispers of hope dance in the night.
Heavy burdens, souls entwined,
Strength in love, solace we find.

With every heartbeat, courage grows,
Through darkest valleys, light still shows.
Embracing trials, we won't break,
For in our hearts, a fire wakes.

Through storms we walk, hand in hand,
Together we rise, together we stand.
Pillars of faith, unwavering, true,
In every heartbeat, I find you.

A tapestry woven from shared pain,
Each thread a bond, love's sweet refrain.
In heart's embrace, we face the test,
Through heavy layers, we find our rest.

In the quiet, resilience blooms,
From shadows cast, hope still looms.
With every heartbeat, we find our way,
In heavy storms, we greet the day.

Lanterns of Resolve

Beneath the veil of dusky skies,
Lanterns flicker, dreams arise.
Guiding stars in twilight's hand,
Lighting paths yet unplanned.

In shadows deep, courage shines,
Each heart a beacon, light defines.
Through storms and trials, we persist,
In every moment, we resist.

Hope like lanterns, warm and bright,
Drawing forth the inner light.
Together shining, we are bold,
In unity, our stories told.

Every challenge, a step to climb,
With every heartbeat, we defy time.
Together we rise, unbowed and free,
In depths of night, we find the key.

The journey long, our spirits soar,
Lanterns guide us to the shore.
Through every struggle, love will weave,
In the tapestry of those who believe.

Resilience Reimagined

In the chaos, beauty lies,
Quiet strength beneath the skies.
Every scar a tale remains,
Resilience born from enduring pains.

Through the ashes, hope takes root,
Branches strong from fragile shoot.
With every challenge, we adapt,
In the dance of life, we're entrapped.

The tides may rise, the winds may howl,
In unity, we'll face the growl.
For in our hearts, a fire burns,
With lessons learned, our spirit turns.

In moments dark, we'll find our light,
Together, we'll carve futures bright.
Resilience, a dance, refined and pure,
In our shared strength, we endure.

Through trials faced, we rise anew,
Every setback leads to the view.
With hope alight and spirits high,
Resilience reimagined, we can fly.

Cadence of the Unyielding

In the rhythm of the brave, we stand,
Echoes of faith, hand in hand.
Every heartbeat, a story retold,
In the cadence of life, legends unfold.

The march of time, relentless and true,
Moments of strength in all that we do.
Through trials faced, our spirits soar,
For united we thrive, forevermore.

Through shadows cast by doubt's lament,
With hope's embrace, we are content.
In unison, we rise, we will cope,
With the cadence of courage, we weave hope.

From whispers soft to thunderous cries,
Our voices lift, breaking the ties.
In every heartbeat, an anthem lies,
The unyielding spirit will always rise.

With every step, we pave the way,
In life's grand symphony, we sway.
Together unbroken, like the sun's ray,
The cadence of the unyielding will stay.

Pulses of Passion

In the quiet night, hearts ignite,
A dance of souls, bathed in light.
Whispers of dreams softly call,
In the rhythm of love, we stand tall.

With each heartbeat, a story unfolds,
A tapestry of warmth, woven in gold.
Moments cherished, lost in time,
In the echoes of laughter, we find our rhyme.

Together we soar, on wings of trust,
Through the storms of life, we find what's just.
In every glance, a world anew,
Our pulses race, forever in view.

The fire within burns fiercely bright,
Guiding us through the darkest night.
With passion's pulse, we chart our way,
In love's embrace, we choose to stay.

Through the highs and lows, we remain,
With endless love, it never wanes.
In this journey, hand in hand,
Our hearts united, forever we stand.

The Beat Goes On

Life's a rhythm, a steady beat,
In every moment, we find our feet.
Through joy and pain, we carry on,
With hope as our guide, the beat goes on.

In the hustle and flow, music plays,
Each note a memory, in sunlit rays.
We dance through the days, side by side,
In the pulse of time, we take our pride.

Echoes of laughter fill the air,
With every heartbeat, we show we care.
Through trials faced, we stand as one,
As the world spins round, our love's not done.

As days turn to nights, stars will shine,
A melody transcends, forever divine.
Together we rise, with spirits high,
In the song of life, we learn to fly.

With every moment, the journey flows,
In the heart's rhythm, true love grows.
Through every chapter, we sing our song,
Together, my dear, the beat goes on.

Songs of the Brave

Amidst the shadows, they stand strong,
The brave heart sings a mighty song.
With courage fierce, they face the fight,
In unity, they conquer the night.

With voices raised, they pierce the air,
For every struggle, they show they care.
Through trials faced, they won't retreat,
In the heart of battle, they find their beat.

For dreams they chase, and hopes they sow,
With every heartbeat, their spirits glow.
Together they rise, through thick and thin,
In the songs of the brave, they find their win.

With steadfast hearts, they forge ahead,
Each note a promise, no fear, no dread.
In the face of doubt, their voices ring,
From the ashes of fear, the brave take wing.

Through storms and trials, they carry on,
In the chorus of life, they've truly won.
Bound by a love that's bold and true,
The songs of the brave shine bright like dew.

The Heart's Horizon

On the edge of dawn, dreams unfold,
With every heartbeat, new stories told.
In the colors of life, we find our way,
Chasing the sun, come what may.

Across the horizon, whispers arise,
In the warmth of hope, we reach for the skies.
With eyes wide open, we embrace the day,
In the heart's horizon, love leads the way.

Each step we take, a journey grand,
Bound by the magic of a loving hand.
With every beat, we live and learn,
In the flame of passion, our spirits burn.

Through valleys low and mountains steep,
In the heart's horizon, our dreams we keep.
With open hearts, we navigate the tide,
In this wondrous journey, we take pride.

As shadows fade and light appears,
In the melody of life, we shed our fears.
Together we stand, come joy or pain,
In the heart's horizon, love will reign.

Echoes of Valor

In shadows deep where heroes tread,
The whispers call, the brave are led.
With hearts aflame, they heed the sound,
In echoes loud, their strength is found.

Through trials faced and fears overcome,
The path is dark, yet courage shuns.
With every step, the light draws near,
In unity, they conquer fear.

The battle cries, a song of old,
Retold in hearts both fierce and bold.
In every scar, a story spun,
Of warriors proud, their race not run.

Through stormy skies and raging seas,
They stand together, strong with ease.
With every breath, their spirits soar,
In valor's name, they fight for more.

In legends vast, their names will weave,
Of those who dared, who chose to believe.
For every echo tells a tale,
Of courage strong that will prevail.

The Brave Within

In quiet moments, whispers stir,
A flicker sparks, intent to spur.
The brave reside in hearts of gold,
In storms of doubt, their light unfolds.

With trembling hands, they face the night,
Embracing shadows, finding light.
A steely gaze, a will so firm,
In every challenge, they discern.

The battles fought, not always seen,
In silent wars, they grow routine.
Yet in the dark, a fire burns,
For every scar, a lesson learns.

Though fears may rise and doubts may creep,
The brave within, their promise keep.
They rise again, with spirits high,
In every fall, they learn to fly.

With hearts adorned in armor bright,
They march ahead, guided by light.
For in their souls, a truth they find,
The bravest heart is love aligned.

Armor of Love

In gentle hands, the heart is shielded,
A sacred bond, where hope is wielded.
Through trials fierce and storms untamed,\nIn armor soft,
their love proclaimed.

With every glance, a vow renewed,
In laughter shared, despair subdued.
They face the world with faith as guide,
With love's embrace, they turn the tide.

Against the odds, they stand as one,
In every battle, they will run.
For love is strong, a force divine,
An armor forged, forever mine.

In whispers sweet and tender grace,
They find their strength in love's embrace.
With open hearts, they choose to fight,
To weave their dreams in shared delight.

Through all adversities they roam,
Together strong, in every home.
For love's bright armor guides the way,
In every night, in every day.

Rising from Ashes

From flames that scorched, a seed takes flight,
In ashes cold, emerges light.
With every end, a brand new start,
From darkness deep, ignites the heart.

With breath anew, they spread their wings,
In hope reborn, the soul still sings.
Through trials set, they stand up tall,
From crumbled past, they heed the call.

The road is long, yet spirits soar,
With lessons learned, they seek for more.
In every scar, a story lies,
Of battles fought beneath the skies.

Through storms of doubt and winds of pain,
They rise again, embrace the rain.
With courage woven into grace,
They carve a path, they find their place.

So let them rise, as phoenix bright,
From ashes cold, into the light.
In every heart, the fire burns,
A testament of life's returns.

Stones of Endurance

In the silence, stones will speak,
Weathered faces, paths unique.
Holding stories, deep and old,
Whispers of the brave and bold.

Through the storms, they choose to stay,
Rooted firm, they find their way.
Each crack tells of time endured,
In their strength, we find assured.

Mossy coats and shadows cast,
Silent witnesses to the past.
In the stillness, strength emerges,
Life's true grit, as hope surges.

Through challenges, they find their course,
Unyielding, they possess a force.
Beneath the weight, they hold their ground,
In their presence, peace is found.

Stones of wisdom, firm and proud,
In each lesson, they enshroud.
With the earth, their bond is grand,
Together strong, they take a stand.

Heartbeats in Harmony

In the quiet of the night,
Two heartbeats dance, pure delight.
Rhythms blend in soft embrace,
Lost in love, they find their place.

Every pulse, a tender call,
In the stillness, they enthrall.
Echoes of a song divine,
Two souls weave, their paths align.

Moments shared, an endless loop,
In their warmth, the world can swoop.
Together they create a tune,
Underneath the silver moon.

With each gaze, the spark ignites,
Passion born in endless nights.
In perfect sync, they rise and fall,
A symphony that binds them all.

Through the storms and sunny days,
These heartbeats share their loving ways.
Side by side, in life's ballet,
A harmony that guides the way.

A Dance of Defiance

In shadows deep, they find their place,
Fierce and bold, they dare to face.
Beneath the chains, their spirits rise,
In every step, a fierce reprise.

With clenched fists, they hit the ground,
Defying odds, their voices sound.
A rhythm born from grit and fight,
Their dance ignites the darkest night.

In every twirl, a story told,
Of broken dreams and hearts of gold.
They leap and bound, unchained, alive,
In defiance, they will thrive.

With blazing fire, they take a stand,
In every clutch, united hand.
With every beat, the spark ignites,
A dance of strength that lights the nights.

Through struggles, they find their grace,
In wild movements, they embrace.
A dance of defiance, proud and true,
In every step, a dream anew.

The Pulse of Persistence

In the chaos, a steady beat,
Persistence shines, it won't retreat.
Through trials faced, they won't give in,
With every setback, they begin.

Each stumble, just a part of growth,
In patience lies their sacred oath.
With eyes fixed on the distant shore,
The pulse of hope beats evermore.

In the struggle, strength is found,
With every effort, courage rises sound.
A rhythm carved in sweat and tears,
The pulse of dreams throughout the years.

Beneath the weight, they stand up tall,
With each heartbeat, they conquer all.
In every challenge, they persist,
Overcoming odds, they can't resist.

Through the journey, lessons learned,
With steadfast hearts, their passion burned.
The pulse of persistence, strong and bright,
Guiding them through the darkest night.

From Cracks to Crescendos

In shadows deep, we often tread,
Through fragile paths where fears are bred.
But every crack holds tales untold,
A symphony of hearts, both brave and bold.

With whispered hopes, we rise anew,
From broken dreams, we seek the true.
Casting doubts to distant shores,
Our spirits soar, forever more.

In moments dim, we find our song,
With every note, we grow more strong.
The echoes of our past ignite,
Transforming pain into pure light.

From cracks emerge the blossoms bright,
Their colors gleam in darkest night.
The crescendos swell, a vibrant chance,
Together we rise, our hearts in dance.

Heartstrings of Resilience

In tangled threads, our stories weave,
Through trials faced, we learn to believe.
With every pull, our courage shows,
A melody of strength that only grows.

Each tear that falls, a lesson gained,
In battles fought, resilience trained.
We strum the chords of hope so bright,
Guided by stars in the endless night.

Our hearts combine, a symphonic beat,
In harmony, we rise from defeat.
Together we stand, a powerful choir,
Fanning the flames of our inner fire.

In life's grand song, we find the key,
Unlocking dreams, setting spirits free.
With heartstrings tied, we craft our fate,
Resilience sings, it never waits.

In the Wake of Trials

When tempests rage and shadows loom,
We chart our course, defiance blooms.
In struggles faced and battles won,
The dawn breaks forth, a new day's begun.

Each struggle forms a stepping stone,
In fractured paths, we find our own.
With hands held high and spirits free,
Together we build our legacy.

In moments dark, we grasp for light,
Finding strength in the heart of night.
With every trial, we unite as one,
In the warmth of hope, no longer undone.

The winds may howl, the waves may crash,
But in our hearts, we hold the flash.
A spark ignites, igniting the fire,
In the wake of trials, we rise higher.

The Light After the Storm

As clouds disperse and daylight breaks,
We find the path that hope awakes.
With every raindrop, lessons learned,
In scars of struggle, our spirit burned.

The gentle hush that follows pain,
A whispered promise to rise again.
In every shadow, a flame resides,
Revealing truths where courage hides.

The sun peeks through with golden rays,
Illuminating our winding ways.
Beneath the weight of heavy skies,
We find our wings, prepared to rise.

In every heart, a story glows,
Of battles fought, and how it grows.
The light after storms shines ever bright,
Guiding us forth into the night.

Beyond Fragility

In shadows deep where whispers dwell,
A heart beats strong beneath the shell.
Through cracks of doubt, the light breaks free,
In fragile strength, we dare to be.

Each scar a story, each tear a song,
In unity, we rise along.
With hopes ignited, we soar so high,
Beyond the limits, we touch the sky.

When storms may rage and tempests roar,
We stand as one, forevermore.
In bonds unbroken, we find our way,
In the night's embrace, we push through the gray.

Through whispers of fear that hold us tight,
We kindle the spark, we ignite the light.
Together we nurture a brave new dawn,
In the garden of dreams, we carry on.

With courage fierce as the stars above,
Resilience blooms, like a gentle dove.
Beyond fragility, we claim our place,
In the heart of the storm, we find our grace.

Winds of Resistance

Across the plains, the wild winds cry,
Echoes of hope that will not die.
Banners of change in the air take flight,
In the heart of the struggle, we stand and fight.

With voices strong, we raise a call,
Against the walls that try to stall.
In every breath, there lies a spark,
Fueled by the dreams that light the dark.

Through valleys deep, we march as one,
Bearing the weight of battles won.
In unity's bond, we find our strength,
Pushing forward, no matter the length.

The winds may roar, the skies may frown,
But with each gust, we'll never back down.
Roots run deep in the soil we share,
In the winds of resistance, we find the air.

With every challenge, we grow anew,
Crafting a world where hope breaks through.
Together we rise, breaking the chains,
In the winds of resistance, our spirit reigns.

Canvas of Courage

With each brushstroke, we tell our tale,
Colors of passion that never pale.
On canvas wide, our dreams take flight,
In the heart of the storm, we find the light.

Shades of bravery, hues of grace,
In every challenge, we find our place.
Painting our visions, we set them free,
In the art of existence, we learn to be.

From dark backgrounds, bright colors bloom,
In the canvas of courage, there's always room.
With fierce expression, we lay it bare,
Creating a world that is strong and rare.

When doubts may whisper, and shadows creep,
We wield our brushes, our promises keep.
In vivid tales of who we are,
We paint with purpose, we reach for stars.

When the canvas beckons, we gather near,
Creating our mantra, our hopes sincere.
In the palette of life, we find our way,
In the canvas of courage, we boldly stay.

Fields of Perseverance

In valleys green where dreams do grow,
The seeds of strength begin to sow.
With every challenge, the roots go deep,
In fields of perseverance, we never sleep.

Through seasons changing, we stand tall,
Weathering storms when the shadows call.
With every sunrise, we greet the day,
In fields of perseverance, we find our way.

Each drop of rain, a lesson learned,
In the soil of patience, our hearts are turned.
Through trials faced and mountains climbed,
In fields of perseverance, we are aligned.

With hands united, we tend the land,
In every struggle, we take a stand.
From roots of courage, our spirits soar,
In the fields of perseverance, we ask for more.

In the harvests gathered, we find our peace,
With gratitude flowing that will not cease.
In the expanse of life where dreams enhance,
In fields of perseverance, we take our chance.

Unbreakable Spirit

In storms we rise, we stand so tall,
With hearts ablaze, we will not fall.
Each challenge faced, a chance to grow,
Our spirit shines; our strength will show.

Through trials hard, we find our way,
Determined souls, we seize the day.
With every step, we learn to fight,
Unbreakable spirit, our guiding light.

When shadows loom, and doubts arise,
We lift our heads and touch the skies.
For in the depths, we find our core,
A fire burns, forever more.

Together we forge, a bond so true,
In unity, we break right through.
No fear can dim this vibrant spark,
Our courage glows, igniting dark.

With open hearts, we march ahead,
In every word, our hopes are spread.
Each victory gained, a tale to tell,
Unbreakable spirit, we rise and dwell.

Chasing the Dawn

In twilight's glow, we find our dreams,
As night surrenders to morning beams.
With each new day, horizons call,
We chase the dawn, we stand up tall.

The stars above, they guide our way,
Each whispered wish, a brighter day.
Through valleys deep, and mountains high,
We seek the light, we learn to fly.

With every moment, the past recedes,
We plant our hopes like scattered seeds.
A canvas bright, we paint it free,
Chasing the dawn, just you and me.

The sun will rise, it never fails,
On unfamiliar paths, we set our sails.
With open minds, we greet the morn,
In every heart, a new day born.

Together we run, hand in hand,
Across the fields, through shifting sand.
With laughter loud and spirits high,
Chasing the dawn, we touch the sky.

Through Shadows to Light

In darkest nights, we search for stars,
The whispers echo from afar.
With every step, we tread the line,
Through shadows deep, our hearts will shine.

Each passing moment, a lesson learned,
In trials faced, our passion burned.
With courage bold, we break the chains,
Through shadows thick, our spirit gains.

The path ahead may twist and turn,
With every setback, we shall discern.
The strength we find in unity,
Through shadows to light, we will be free.

Together we rise, dispelling doubt,
With open minds, we'll figure out.
The dawn will break, the day will rise,
Through shadows to light, we claim the skies.

With every heartbeat, truth unfolds,
Stories written in whispers bold.
Through darkness deep, our voices sing,
From shadowed paths, to light we bring.

The Power Within

In silence lies a raging storm,
A fire's glow, both fierce and warm.
With every breath, we draw from deep,
The power within, a promise we keep.

Through trials faced, our strengths ignite,
Emerging fierce, we shine so bright.
With open hearts, we claim our ground,
The power within, forever profound.

Each moment whispers, "You are strong,"
A melody, a timeless song.
We rise anew, no fear of flight,
The power within, our guiding light.

In unity, we find our voice,
Together we soar, we make our choice.
The strength we hold, it will not fade,
The power within, our plans well laid.

So let us march, with heads held high,
Through every storm, we'll touch the sky.
With faith unbroken and hearts that sing,
The power within, our everything.

Resilience in Bloom

In the garden of moments, we stand,
Nurtured by hope, a guiding hand.
Through storms and shadows, we find our way,
Petals of strength in the light of day.

With roots entwined in the earth's embrace,
We rise anew, with unwavering grace.
Each trial faced, a lesson learned,
In the heart's fire, true passion burned.

Soft whispers of courage in the breeze,
A symphony of dreams that never cease.
With every blossom, a story told,
Of perseverance, brave and bold.

In the dance of seasons, we sway,
With the rhythm of life, come what may.
Through time's embrace, we flourish and thrive,
In the face of despair, we truly arrive.

As petals unfurl in the warm sunlight,
We stand together, ready for flight.
With each new dawn, our spirits bloom,
In the garden of courage, there's always room.

Courageous Rhythms

Beats of the heart echo in the night,
Guiding the soul in its soaring flight.
With every challenge, we hold the line,
In the face of fear, our stars align.

Through valleys deep and mountains steep,
In the shadows, where the brave do leap.
The rhythm of life is a fierce drum,
Calling us forth, we won't succumb.

With every step, a story unfolds,
In the tapestry woven, courage holds.
In harmony's embrace, we stand tall,
Together in faith, we conquer all.

A dance of resilience at every turn,
In the fire of trials, our spirits burn.
With beating hearts, we find our way,
In the cadence of hope, we shall stay.

In the symphony of life, we sing along,
With the strength of many, we are strong.
In each courageous rhythm, we find our truth,
In the dance of existence, we embrace our youth.

The Unyielding Pulse

In the silence, a pulse beats strong,
An unyielding rhythm where we belong.
Through trials and tempests, we boldly tread,
With strength anew, we follow the thread.

Each heartbeat whispers tales of might,
A journey forged in the darkest night.
With courage ignited, we find our way,
In the heartbeat of hope, we proudly stay.

Against the odds, we rise and soar,
With spirits unbroken, we seek for more.
Every challenge faced becomes our song,
In the pulse of life, we all belong.

Through the storm's roar and the stillness, too,
In the dance of persistence, we break through.
With every thud, a testament grows,
In the journey of life, resilience shows.

With unity pulsing, we echo as one,
In the tapestry woven, our lifeline spun.
With the unyielding pulse, we push on through,
Embracing the journey, forever true.

Echoes of Fortitude

In the valleys deep where shadows lay,
Echoes of strength guide our way.
With every whisper, fear takes flight,
In the heart's courage, we find the light.

Across the mountains, our spirits soar,
Through trials faced, we seek for more.
In the cadence of hope, we rise,
With fortitude's echo, we touch the skies.

In the silence, resilience speaks,
Through every struggle, the heart seeks.
With boldness wrapped in a fierce embrace,
We carve our path, we find our place.

The whispers of past, lessons in bloom,
In the shadows, we dispel the gloom.
With every heartbeat, echoes resound,
In the strength of spirit, our truth is found.

Together we stand, a steadfast crew,
In the dance of life, we break through.
With echoes of fortitude ringing clear,
We embrace the journey, united, no fear.

When Hope Takes Flight

In the gentle dawn of day,
Dreams begin to light the way.
With every step, the heart can soar,
A whisper echoes, 'Hope for more.'

The skies transform, a canvas grand,
With colors soft, like grains of sand.
Let courage fuel the wings so bright,
As hope ascends and takes to flight.

Through tempests fierce and shadows long,
The spirit hums a hopeful song.
With each new dawn, it starts anew,
Unfurling dreams in skies of blue.

Together we can dare to dream,
In unity, we craft our seam.
With every heartbeat, joy ignites,
Our souls entwined, as hope takes flight.

So grasp the light, hold it tight,
For in our hearts, we find our might.
Each challenge faced, a chance to rise,
When hope alights, it never dies.

The Anatomy of Healing

In silence deep, a whisper flows,
A tender touch where spirit grows.
Within the ache, a strength we find,
In brokenness, we're redefined.

The heart learns slowly, beat by beat,
Through cracks and scars, it finds its seat.
Each moment spent in quiet grace,
Unfolds the truth we dare to face.

With hands that nurture and console,
We stitch together every hole.
From wounds so raw, new life appears,
In healing's dance, we drown our fears.

The journey winds through joy and pain,
Yet through the storms, we learn to gain.
Embrace the warmth that time provides,
For in each scar, a beauty hides.

So let us tread this path in trust,
As hope and love renew the dust.
With every breath, we craft a song,
In the anatomy of healing, we belong.

Embracing Fire

In the blaze of life, we find our flame,
A spark ignites, refusing to tame.
With passion's breath, we dance and spin,
Embrace the fire that dwells within.

Each flicker tells a tale of old,
Of dreams pursued, of hearts so bold.
Through trials faced, our spirits rise,
In every blaze, a chance to advise.

The heat may burn, yet we are strong,
With fiery hearts, we'll carry on.
Through every challenge, hold on tight,
In shadows cast, we seek the light.

To face the flames, we shed our fears,
With every alight, a soul appears.
Transformation waits in every spark,
Embracing fire, igniting the dark.

So let your heart be fiercely bright,
In every trial, find your light.
Unleash the passion, rise and strive,
For in embracing fire, we come alive.

Songs of the Indomitable

From valleys low to mountains high,
The indomitable spirit cries.
With voices raised, we sing our truth,
In every age, in every youth.

Through storms and trials, we will stand,
Together strong, hand in hand.
In harmony, our hearts unite,
With courage bright, we face the night.

The rhythm flows, a beating heart,
In every soul, we play our part.
The songs we craft, a legacy,
Of hope and strength, of unity.

When shadows loom and doubt may creep,
We'll lift our song, our promise keep.
In every note, a story told,
Of battles fought, and hearts of gold.

So let the music fill the air,
In every corner, everywhere.
For we are strong, indomitable still,
With songs of courage, we fulfill.

Roots of Resolve

In the soil, dreams take hold,
Whispers of stories yet untold.
Through struggles, we find our way,
Nurtured by hope, day by day.

Branches stretch towards the sky,
With every storm, we learn to fly.
Our roots run deep, steadfast and true,
Bound by the love that we pursue.

Within us lies an endless strength,
To face the trials at any length.
For every setback, we will rise,
With courage lighting up the skies.

Together, strong, we will stand tall,
In unity, we will not fall.
From every struggle, wisdom grows,
As the spirit of resilience flows.

In the heart of every challenge,
Lies the spark that fuels the balance.
We thrive in darkness, find our light,
For in our roots, we hold the fight.

Surge of the Brave

A thunderous roar ignites the night,
Courageous hearts prepared to fight.
With every step, the ground does quake,
Voices rise; it's time to wake.

Boundless courage, unyielding flame,
Pushing forward, no hint of shame.
We are the tides, unstoppable force,
Guided by purpose, we chart our course.

Through the storm, we will not bend,
With each other, we will transcend.
Honor and valor pave our way,
Together, we find strength to stay.

Each heartbeat echoes in the fight,
A surge of bravery, pure and bright.
With steadfast hearts, we claim the day,
In unity, we'll find our way.

The world may tremble, but we will stand,
With open hearts and outstretched hands.
For in the struggle, bonds are forged,
The surge of the brave, our spirits soared.

Miracles in Motion

In every step, a spark ignites,
With open eyes, we reach new heights.
The world unfolds, a canvas bright,
Miracles dance in morning light.

Time flows like a gentle stream,
Each moment holds a cherished dream.
We weave our stories, thread by thread,
With every heartbeat, life is fed.

Amidst the chaos, beauty blooms,
In whispered love, the heart consumes.
Every action, a rippling tide,
Miracles found when hope abides.

In laughter shared and kindness shown,
We build the seeds of love we've sown.
With open hearts, we pave the way,
For miracles soar and never sway.

Together, we rise, as one we roam,
In every moment, we find our home.
The world around us shines and glows,
In miracles, our spirit grows.

Heartbeats of Determination

Every heartbeat calls us near,
In the silence, we can hear.
With steadfast will and eyes so bright,
We embrace the dark, we chase the light.

With every challenge, we find grace,
A rhythm strong, we'll set the pace.
Through trials faced and mountains high,
Our hearts will sing and never die.

In every struggle, strength is born,
Through pain and strife, we rise reborn.
With courage wrapped in passion's glow,
Determination leads us where to go.

The journey's long, yet worth the fight,
With every heartbeat, we ignite.
For in the grit, our spirits soar,
As we open every hopeful door.

Together, we create the sound,
Of heartbeats strong, forever bound.
In unity, we'll stand and roar,
With determination, we'll restore.

Heart of Iron

In shadows deep, where silence lies,
A beating heart, strong as the skies.
Forged in the flames of every trial,
Its strength, unwavering, every mile.

Resilient spirit, fierce and bright,
With courage found in darkest night.
Steel and fire, passion's embrace,
In the heart of iron, find your place.

From scars emerged, a warrior's song,
In unity, we shall stand strong.
With every heartbeat, vows we renew,
In this iron heart, hope rings true.

Let the storm rage, let the winds howl,
In this safe haven, we shall prowl.
Honest whispers, echoes of pain,
In the heart of iron, we remain.

Together we rise, together we soar,
In the heartbeat's rhythm, we explore.
Bound by strength, and souls entwined,
The heart of iron, forever kind.

Bridges of Bravery

Across the void, where fears collide,
We build our paths, with hope as guide.
Each step a mark on this unyielding way,
Bridges of bravery, come what may.

With hands outstretched, we grasp the light,
Facing the shadows, standing upright.
Strength in numbers, voices ring clear,
On bridges of bravery, we banish fear.

From terror's grasp, we break away,
Unified march, brighter the day.
In every heartbeat, courage is found,
On bridges of bravery, we stand our ground.

Waves may crash, and storms may come,
Yet through the trials, we'll never succumb.
Walking together, hand in hand,
Strength on bridges, together we stand.

Let sirens sing and mountains shake,
In unity's name, our spirits awake.
With stories to tell, and battles to share,
We cross the bridges of bravery, unaware.

Resonance of Resolve

In echoes soft, a promise starts,
Whispers of strength, within our hearts.
Resonance found in every sigh,
The fire within, we can't deny.

Through valleys low and mountains high,
In the depths of doubt, we reach for the sky.
Each heartbeat strong, clarity brings,
In resonance, the courage sings.

Bonded by dreams, a circle of trust,
Desires ignited, in love we must.
United we stand, come what may,
In the resonance of resolve, we'll find our way.

Let challenges rise, like tides on the shore,
With every breath, we'll strive for more.
A symphony strong, an unbreakable roll,
In the resonance of resolve, we find our soul.

Through storms we weather, bright stars we chase,
In the echoes of hope, we find our place.
Together we bind, heart to heart,
In the resonance of resolve, we'll never part.

Fists of Compassion

With fists of compassion, we break the chains,
Together we rise, through losses and gains.
Strength wrapped in kindness, a powerful shield,
In battles of love, our hearts are revealed.

In gentle touches, we raise our voice,
Fists of compassion, we make our choice.
To fight for the lost, the broken, the meek,
In unity's spirit, we rise to speak.

From whispers of hope, our actions combine,
In every heart, a strength divine.
With every heartbeat, our purpose stands,
Fists of compassion, together we can.

Through struggles shared, we break the mold,
With tender heartbeats, our stories unfold.
A warrior's embrace, in shadows we shine,
Fists of compassion, in love we align.

So let us unite, with hands open wide,
In compassion's name, let's turn the tide.
With strength of the heart, we'll forever endure,
In fists of compassion, we will be sure.

Discovering the Stronghold

In the mist of dawn's first light,
We seek a place of peace and might.
A fortress built from dreams so bold,
Where whispers of the past unfold.

Through shadows cast by doubt and fear,
We find the strength when we draw near.
Within these walls, our spirits rise,
A beacon shining in the skies.

Each stone laid with the hands of time,
Echoes of hope in every rhyme.
Together we will break the mold,
In unity, our hearts we hold.

With every challenge that we face,
We carve our name, we find our place.
In this stronghold, hand in hand,
We'll forge a path, we'll make our stand.

Let storms approach and darkness call,
Within these walls, we shall not fall.
For in our hearts, a fire burns bright,
In discovering our stronghold's light.

Whirlwinds of Will

In the eye of the tempest's roar,
We discover what we're fighting for.
The winds of doubt may swirl and spin,
Yet deep inside, we know we'll win.

Every gust that pulls us down,
Is a chance to rise, not wear a frown.
With resolve, we face the storm,
In whirlwinds our true selves are born.

Through chaos, we learn to steer,
Understanding that strength is near.
Each challenge bravely we confront,
In courage, we will ever hunt.

Like leaves that twirl yet stay intact,
Our spirits soar, we won't retract.
For in these whirlwinds, we shall find,
The will to grow, the heart to bind.

So let the winds come fierce and wild,
We venture forth, the free-spirited child.
In every swirl, our dreams ignite,
Through whirlwinds of will, we find our light.

Guardians of the Heart

In the silence of the midnight hour,
We gather strength, we bloom like flower.
Guardians stand, both proud and wise,
Holding love beneath the skies.

With every heartbeat, bonds are forged,
In unity, our spirits are gorged.
Sharing laughter, sharing tears,
Guardians rise above our fears.

Through the trials that life may send,
Together we will always tend.
The light that shines from deep within,
Guardians of heart, we always win.

Each melody a sacred vow,
Together we shall live in now.
No storm can shake this sacred art,
For we are guardians of the heart.

In moments frail, in times of strife,
We find the joy that gives us life.
In every pulse, a love so true,
The guardians of hope, me and you.

The Strength to Stand Tall

In the valley where shadows dwell,
We gather courage, weave our spell.
With every step, we learn to rise,
The strength within, a great surprise.

Though mountains loom and skies turn gray,
We lift our chin, we find our way.
In every stumble, we learn to crawl,
Until we're ready to stand tall.

With voices united, we sing our song,
In harmony, we all belong.
Through trials faced, our spirit soars,
In unity, we open doors.

Every setback is a chance to learn,
With fire ignited, we brightly burn.
Through stormy nights and sunny days,
In finding strength, we leave a blaze.

So here we stand, both fierce and free,
In this life, just let it be.
With every heartbeat, we answer the call,
With the strength to rise, the strength to stand tall.

Heartstrings of Hope

In the silence, whispers start,
Dreams awaken, a brand new heart.
Beneath the stars, we find the way,
Guided by hope, we seize the day.

Through the shadows, light will shine,
Weaving courage, thread by line.
In unity, our spirits soar,
With every step, we yearn for more.

Holding dreams both near and dear,
In every heartbeat, love draws near.
As morning breaks, the dawn unfolds,
A tapestry of stories told.

In every trial, strength we'll find,
A bond unbroken, hearts entwined.
With every tear, we rise anew,
Painting life in vibrant hue.

So let us sing, our voices strong,
In harmony, we all belong.
A dance of hope, a timeless song,
Together, we can right the wrong.

The Strength Beneath

In quiet moments, power grows,
A gentle force, nobody knows.
Roots run deep, through stone and sand,
In stillness, strength takes a stand.

With every challenge, walls may rise,
Yet in our hearts, the spirit flies.
Through storms and trials, we hold tight,
Together, we turn dark to light.

Beneath the waves, the ocean's grace,
Resilience blooms in every place.
When faced with doubt, we'll stand as one,
Our journey forged, never undone.

For in the struggle, we will see,
The strength that binds you next to me.
A testament of grit and will,
In every silence, hear the thrill.

So lift your heart and face the dawn,
In every battle, we carry on.
Unified, we chart our course,
Embracing life in all its force.

Flames of Tenacity

From ashes rise, a spark ignites,
With fervent flames, we take our flights.
In every heart, the fire grows,
A burning passion that freely flows.

Through shadows cast, we chase the glow,
Refusing to yield, refusing to slow.
In every failure, lessons learned,
A tempered spirit, brightly burned.

With every struggle, embers plead,
A flame of courage, planted seed.
We rise like phoenixes from the ground,
In solidarity, our strength is found.

Against the winds, our will is strong,
With hopeful hearts, we sing our song.
Through trials fierce, we forge ahead,
In unity, let our voices spread.

So fan the flames, let passion soar,
In every heartbeat, seek for more.
Together, we'll break through the night,
With flames of tenacity, ignite the light.

Grit and Grace

In the calm and in the storm,
We balance strength, a perfect form.
With every stumble, elegance found,
In every heartbeat, grace resounds.

Through muddy paths, we walk with pride,
With grit and grace, right by our side.
For every challenge that we face,
We rise, resilient, with steadfast grace.

In the quiet moments, courage blooms,
Lighting up the darkest rooms.
With every step, our spirits dance,
A testament to life's expanse.

So join the journey, hand in hand,
With hearts united, we will stand.
Through trials tough, our spirits race,
In grit and grace, we'll find our place.

So let the world see our embrace,
In every struggle, find our pace.
With grit ignited and spirits high,
We'll paint our legacy in the sky.

The Tides of Tenacity

In storms we find our strength anew,
With waves that crash, we stand so true.
Each setback sends us back to shore,
But deep within, we crave for more.

The moon commands the ocean's dance,
While we embrace each second chance.
For in the ebb, there lies a flow,
And from the depths, we rise and grow.

Through trials faced and battles fought,
Our will ignites, a fire sought.
With every surge, we learn to sway,
Resilience blooms in light of day.

The tides may shift, the paths unsure,
Yet steadfast hearts, they will endure.
For in the waves, our tales are spun,
A song of hope, forever sung.

So let the winds of change then blow,
For we are anchored, strong, and whole.
In every rise, in every fall,
We stand united, brave for all.

Foundations of Fortitude

In darkened days when shadows creep,
We build our hopes, our dreams to keep.
Each stone laid down with care and grace,
A tribute to the human race.

Through trials that would break the weak,
Our spirits soar, our hearts will speak.
With every choice, our roots grow deep,
As fortitude, we vow to keep.

The ground may shake, the skies may roar,
But still we rise, we seek for more.
In unity, we find our blend,
With foundations strong, we will not bend.

Through grit and grace, we shape our fate,
With loving hands, we elevate.
The walls we build, they stand so tall,
In strength we find we conquer all.

For every doubt that dares to bloom,
We scatter light, dispel the gloom.
Our hearts a fortress, safe and sound,
In courage's arms, we've found our ground.

The Power to Soar

With wings of dreams, we take to flight,
Chasing the dawn, embracing light.
The winds of change, they lift us high,
As we remember how to fly.

In whispered hopes, our spirits rise,
We break the chains, we touch the skies.
With every leap and every fall,
We gather strength, we heed the call.

The horizon calls, a beacon bright,
Fueling our fire, igniting the night.
Through valleys deep and mountains tall,
We find our voice, we stand for all.

In heart and mind, the power grows,
A phoenix born from ash and blows.
With every breath, we dare to seek,
The sky is ours, the future speaks.

So let us dance on clouds of blue,
Embracing all that we can do.
For in our hearts, the truth we store,
Is simply this: We were meant to soar.

Threads of Grit

In the tapestry of dreams we weave,
Each thread of grit, we dare believe.
Though challenges may fray our seams,
We stitch together all our dreams.

With needle sharp and heart so bold,
We craft our stories, rich and gold.
Through trials faced, our hands do ache,
But in the pain, our bonds we make.

The fabric strong, it holds us tight,
In darkest hours, we find our light.
With every knot, our strength is shown,
In unity, we have all grown.

Through storms and trials, we remain,
Resilient threads, we rise again.
In every weave, a tale unfolds,
A testament to hearts of gold.

So let us cherish every stitch,
In life's grand quilt, each perfect niche.
With threads of grit that we endure,
Our legacy, forever pure.

The Will to Rise

In shadows deep, where doubts reside,
The spirit yearns, with strength to bide.
Through trials faced, we learn to cope,
With every fall, we cling to hope.

A flicker shines, ignites the night,
From ashes cold, we seek the light.
With grit and grace, we stand anew,
Defying odds, we push on through.

The mountain looms, a daunting sight,
Yet step by step, we claim our flight.
With whispered dreams, we rise again,
Refusing still to bow to pain.

In unity, our voices soar,
Together strong, forevermore.
Each heart a beacon, fierce and proud,
We find our strength amidst the crowd.

Above the storms, we plant our feet,
With open hearts, we learn to greet.
The dawn of hope, a brand new prize,
Together bound, we will arise.

A Storm Within

In silence lies a brewing force,
A tempest fierce, it charts its course.
Winds of change begin to howl,
As shadows dance, the darkness growls.

With thunder's voice, my heart it shakes,
The inner tide, it ebbs and breaks.
Each fear unleashed, like lightning's flash,
A clash of souls, the spirits smash.

Yet in this storm, a glimpse of calm,
An eye of peace, a soothing balm.
Through raging waves, I sail the night,
For even storms must yield to light.

The battle rages, tempers flare,
But in the chaos, strength lays bare.
I've weathered pain, embraced the strife,
For every storm, it shapes my life.

As raindrops cleanse, the earth is reborn,
I find my wings, though battered, worn.
In every tempest, I will grow,
For from the storm, new seeds will sow.

Wings of the Unbroken

With every scar that marks my skin,
A story told of where I've been.
I spread my wings, though bruised and torn,
In flight, I find my strength reborn.

The skies are vast, the wind it calls,
I rise above, despite my falls.
Each challenge faced, a lesson learned,
With every flame, my spirit burned.

The world may try to clip my seams,
Yet in my heart, I hold my dreams.
Like phoenix born from ashes bleak,
Resilience soars, the brave will speak.

With hope as fuel, I chase the sun,
The path ahead is never done.
In every storm, I find my grace,
The wings of courage, I embrace.

Though shadows loom and doubts may creep,
In faith, I trust, my heart shall leap.
For in the flight, I find my place,
The unbroken dance, a timeless space.

The Heart's Odyssey

A journey starts within the soul,
Through winding paths, we seek the goal.
With every beat, the pulse of dreams,
The heart it stirs, in quiet streams.

With echoes soft, past whispers call,
Memories weave through every hall.
The laughter shared, the tears we shed,
Each step a bridge, where love is spread.

Through valleys low and mountains high,
In every challenge, we learn to fly.
The compass points to all that's true,
In every heart, a world anew.

Though storms may rage and doubts may bloom,
The heart's resolve can pierce the gloom.
Each scar a tale of strength embraced,
An odyssey, no time can waste.

United by the paths we've crossed,
In every heart, no love is lost.
Together we rise, forever free,
The journey shared, our legacy.

The Heart's Resurgence

In the shadows deep and wide,
Whispers of hope abide.
Through the cracks, light will creep,
Awakening dreams from sleep.

With every tear that falls,
Strength echoes through the walls.
A heart once bruised and worn,
Finds its beat in a new dawn.

Fading memories of despair,
Transform to triumph in the air.
A symphony of scars and grace,
A testament to the heart's embrace.

Embers glow where ashes lay,
Guiding the lost on their way.
With resilience as our song,
Together, we will stand strong.

In the dance of fate we find,
All our dreams intertwined.
From the ruins of the past,
A love reborn, vast and steadfast.

Flame Beneath the Ashes

In the stillness, embers glow,
Whispers of what we once know.
From silence, a fire takes flight,
Kindling dreams in the night.

Ashes scattered, tales untold,
A spark ignites the brave and bold.
Through the darkness, passions rise,
Lighting paths to the skies.

Within the chaos, hope remains,
Fighting through the weight of chains.
Flames dance like a wild breeze,
Bringing warmth and inner peace.

With each flicker, hearts ignite,
Transforming shadows into light.
From the struggle, strength we gain,
A flame beneath the ashes remains.

Through the storm, we are reborn,
In the love that we have worn.
Resilience fuels our flame anew,
As life unfolds in every hue.

Grit and Grace

Through the valleys, we will tread,
With courage as our thread.
Tattered sails against the gales,
In our hearts, a tale prevails.

Stumbling paths and heavy loads,
Gritty hearts forge new roads.
With every fall, we stand again,
Resilient spirits rise from pain.

Grace in moments, fierce yet kind,
Finding strength within the blind.
Through every battle, every strife,
We carve our destiny in life.

With gentle hands, we mend our souls,
Breathing hope as courage unfolds.
In the dance of time and space,
We embody grit and grace.

From the ashes, we'll arise,
With fire burning in our eyes.
Together, through the storm we chase,
A journey filled with grit and grace.

Bridges Built from Pain

From the depths of sorrow's well,
A story rises, hearts to tell.
Each crack and crevice forms a map,
Of journeys taken, fate's own trap.

With every tear, a bridge we weave,
Connecting souls who dare believe.
Pain transforms, a pathway bright,
Leading us to love's pure light.

In the shadows, strength is born,
Together through the night we're sworn.
A tapestry of trials faced,
Bridges built and lives embraced.

From suffering's depths, we find our way,
Building bonds that never sway.
Hope shines through every seam,
We rise together, stronger as a dream.

With open hearts, let's span the gap,
Finding solace in love's map.
We're architects of joy and pain,
Creating bridges time won't feign.

The Pulse of Possibility

In the stillness of dawn's light,
Dreams awaken, taking flight.
Whispers of hope fill the air,
Embrace the chance, be aware.

Every heartbeat stirs the soul,
A dance of futures, brave and whole.
Paths of wonder come alive,
In this moment, we all thrive.

Open your eyes to the vast unknown,
In the garden of life, seeds are sown.
With every step, the world expands,
Hold your dreams with steady hands.

The stars align, a guiding light,
Each choice matters, day or night.
The pulse of possibility calls,
Rise up and embrace it all.

In the echoes of our chase,
We find strength, we find grace.
Together we weave the grand design,
In every heart, the spirit shines.

Wings of the Resilient

Through valleys deep and mountains high,
The resilient rise, they touch the sky.
With grit and grace, they soar on high,
Through storms, they learn to fly.

In sharp winds, they bend but don't break,
Every challenge is a chance to wake.
Feathers of hope in a world so wild,
The heart of the brave, forever a child.

As dawn paints gold on the horizon,
They spread their wings, a new season.
With every struggle, they find their way,
In the fiercest night, they await the day.

The world may try to cage their dreams,
But through the cracks, their spirit beams.
Boldly they venture, far and wide,
With wings of courage as their guide.

In unity, they rise and sing,
Together, they face what life may bring.
The wings of the resilient, strong and free,
In every heart, they carry a key.

Heartbeats of Metal

In the city where the machines hum,
Life pulses loud, a steady drum.
Iron hearts, they stand so tall,
From steel and sweat, they will not fall.

With every clang, a story told,
Threads of strength in shades of gold.
The rhythm of progress, fierce and true,
In the forge of dreams, they push through.

Amidst the grind, sparks light the way,
Each heartbeat a rhythm that won't sway.
They craft the future, bold and bright,
In shadows cast, they ignite the light.

Through trials faced, they build anew,
In every flaw, life's beauty grew.
The heartbeats of metal echo strong,
In unity, they all belong.

As the ages pass, they mark their ground,
With every pulse, a strength profound.
Together they rise, a symphony,
In the heart of metal, life runs free.

Rivers of Resolve

Flowing through valleys, deep and wide,
The rivers of resolve never subside.
With currents fierce, they carve their path,
Through challenges faced, they find their wrath.

Gentle yet mighty, they twist and turn,
In every bend, lessons to learn.
Bridges built on dreams so bold,
Stories of courage in every fold.

Though obstacles rise like stones in the way,
The rivers push forth, never to sway.
With hope as the compass, they journey on,
In waters of resolve, new dawns are drawn.

The echoes of nature, a song of the free,
Flowing together, in harmony, we see.
With hearts like rivers, unyielding and strong,
We chart our course, in the world's vast throng.

Through valleys shadowed and mountains high,
The rivers of resolve reach for the sky.
In every challenge, they find their grace,
A testament to strength we all embrace.

Beyond the Shadows

In the stillness of the night,
Whispers dance on the air,
Dreams emerge from the dark,
Flickering light, hope laid bare.

Footsteps echo on the ground,
Guided by a silent trust,
Beyond the shadows, we are found,
In the dawn, we rise from dust.

Each heartbeat tells a tale,
Of journeys long and wide,
Weaving through the vale,
With courage as our guide.

Together we will soar,
Above the fears that bind,
Breaking through the door,
Embracing what we find.

Beyond the shadows cast,
A world awaits our grace,
In the light, we are vast,
Together we embrace.

Heartbeats of Triumph

Hear the echoes of our fight,
In the stillness of the morn,
Resilience shining bright,
From struggles, we are born.

Every heartbeat tells a story,
Of battles fought and won,
Embodying our glory,
The journey has begun.

Through valleys deep and wide,
We rise above the pain,
With hope, we shall abide,
And dance in the rain.

Together, hand in hand,
We'll weather every storm,
In unity we stand,
Creating our own form.

With each step, we rejoice,
In the power of our dreams,
Echoing our voice,
In heartbeats, strength redeems.

Resilient Rhythms

Feel the pulse of the ground,
As we move to the beat,
Resilient rhythms found,
In moments bittersweet.

Through the noise and the clatter,
We find our sacred space,
Each note a gentle matter,
Each silence, filled with grace.

Like a river, we flow,
Through valleys made of woes,
With strength we do grow,
And courage freely shows.

In harmony, we unite,
Voices strong and clear,
Together, we ignite,
The dreams we hold so dear.

Let the music guide our way,
In the heart of the fray,
With resilient rhythms play,
Creating brighter day.

The Fires Within

Beneath the surface lies a flame,
A spark that starts to grow,
In the darkness, we proclaim,
The fires within us glow.

With every challenge faced,
We stoke the burning light,
In the heart, there's no haste,
For within, we hold the might.

Through the ashes, we will rise,
Transforming grief to gold,
Embracing all the cries,
And stories left untold.

Our passions fiercely blaze,
Illuminating the night,
In their warm embrace,
We discover endless light.

So let us tend our fires,
With every breath we take,
For within, our hearts are pyres,
Creating paths we make.

Milton Keynes UK
Ingram Content Group UK Ltd.
UKHW021629011224
451755UK00010B/532